Britney

by Jo Hurley

SCHOLASTIC INC.

New York   Toronto   London   Auckland   Sydney   Mexico City   New Delhi   Hong Kong

This book is unauthorized and is not sponsored by Britney Spears, her representatives, or anyone involved with her.

Front Cover: Marc Royce/Corbis Outline; Back Cover: Marc Royce/Corbis Outline; Page 1: Ron Davis/Shooting Star; Page 2: James Smeal/Ron Galella Ltd; Page 3: James Smeal/Ron Galella Ltd; Page 4: Henry Lamb/Ron Galella Ltd (top); Page 4: Paul Fenton/Shooting Star (bottom); Page 5: James Smeal/Ron Galella Ltd; Page 6: James Smeal/Ron Galella Ltd; Page 7: Jeff Slocomb/Corbis Outline; Page 8: Robin Platzer; Page 9: Kevin Estrada/Retna; Page 10: Steve Sands/Corbis Outline; Page 11: Dave Hogan/Retna; Page 12: Gilbert Flores/Celebrity Photo; Page 13: Gilbert Flores/Celebrity Photo; Page 14: Paul Fenton/Shooting Star; Page 15: Ron Davis/Shooting Star; Page 16: Steve Granitz/Retna.

ISBN 0-439-22222-2

Designed by Peter Koblish

12 11 10 9 8 7 6 5 4 3   0 1 2 3 4 5 6/0
Printed in the U.S.A.
First Scholastic printing, September 2000

TABLE OF CONTENTS

INTRODUCTION

Ready, Set, BIO!

"I'm having the time of my life. All this hard work has paid off."

[*People* magazine]

Have you ever had a dream that you wanted to come true? Britney Spears knows all about dreams. She's making history right now watching her dreams happen. "I always wanted to be a singer ever since I was little, and now here I am doing the things I love most."

Britney loves singing.

Britney loves dancing.

Britney loves being on top of the world.

That's a good thing — because Britney has been sitting on top of the world for the last two incredible, award-winning years. Since 1998, she has traveled and performed all over the globe while her debut album and its videos rocketed to the top of the charts. The most amazing part: Britney is not slowing down. If anything, this superstar is just getting warmed up.

In early 1999, Britney blew fans away with the record-breaking, history-making number-one smash album . . . *Baby One More Time*. She is the youngest female artist ever to hit *Billboard*'s Top 200 chart with a number-one album and a number-one single at the same time. *TRL* (MTV's *Total Request Live*) called Britney their "patron saint," because in 1999 fans requested Britney's videos more than almost anyone else's. In six short months she went from being an opening act for 'N Sync to headlining her very own concerts and events in some of the largest arenas across the world. When . . . *Baby One More Time* went on sale, Britney went from having almost no fans to having an on-line fan club and Web site that received 10,000 hits in its first week.

Now, her new album, *Oops! . . . I Did It Again*, is hitting the charts and she's on another amazing tour.

Can you say wow?

Of course, Britney's success didn't happen overnight. She's been onstage since she was a teeny tot back in the town of Kentwood, Louisiana. Her road to pop fame and fun has been paved with some speed bumps, endless hours recording and performing, and way too much time away from home. But Britney never let hard knocks get her down. Tough times made her *more* determined than ever to pursue her dreams. "I just want to grow as a person with each new experience, good or bad," she told MTV. In a *Forbes* magazine cover story, Britney admitted that she's stocked up on *major* optimism about her career. "Once you have fans, they want you to succeed. I don't think I'll have any problems."

Britney believes she's really not much different from those fans. "I'm just like any other teenager out there. I'm just doing different things." Those "different things" include topping the *Billboard* charts, winning an American Music Award, being nominated for a Grammy, and sweeping the MTV Europe Music Awards, but all that success has not gone to her head, nor has it changed the kind of person she is.

Britney still gets homesick, still worries about dating, and still gets zits.

And after the *Oops! . . . I Did It Again* concert lights dim . . .

After *TRL* calls it a wrap . . .

After *Teen* has its final photo op . . .

Britney Spears will still be sitting on top of the world, dreaming her dreams, and doing what she loves best.

CHAPTER 1
A Whole Lotta Love

"I always try to remember that everything is going to be all right as long as I stay grounded and remember that I am surrounded by love."

[MTV Online]

In Britney's hometown of Kentwood, Louisiana, life moves at an easy pace. The state prides itself on yummy dishes like country-fried catfish and jambalaya (catfish, shrimp, rice, and spices), a lush landscape, and the best music. Louisiana is a genuine musical melting pot, with a legacy that includes jazz, blues, Cajun, rock 'n' roll, gospel, and classical all rolled into one.

What better place to launch the career of a musical princess?

The town of Kentwood shows big-time pride in their superstar "daughter." For Britney, having hometown fans is like having a crew of cheerleaders constantly rallying for her. Kentwood's Mayor Bobby Gill counts himself as Britney's number-one fan. According to the *New Orleans Times-Picayune*, Gill listens to her album while he works.

The fantastic stories of Britney's loving Louisiana neighbors don't stop there. Boys, girls, moms, and grandmoms get in their cars and trek to Britney's sold-out concerts. One Kentwood bank teller proudly displays a signed photograph of Britney in her office. Nyla's Burger Basket restaurant up the road says it's the Spearses' "favorite dining spot." No matter where you turn, everyone stands behind this native daughter.

The admiration is mutual. Britney gushes, "I love where I come from." She admitted to *People* magazine, "If I wasn't in love with my job and in love with my music, I would be homesick and going crazy."

Britney believes that growing up in a small town the size of Kentwood — population 2,500 — helped to establish a solid belief in herself and her abilities. "In a small town, you tend to have more values — you can take your time growing up." Although Britney's career is moving at a breakneck pace, she wants to savor every special moment.

Since she was raised Southern Baptist, religion plays an important part in Britney's life, too. She's grateful for this because her spiritual beliefs ensure that she get won't a big head as she dives into the music scene. Britney knows how to stay focused on her goals — and her natural gifts. No matter how far concert tours pull her away from Louisiana, she will always be a home-sweet-homebody.

Stars in Her Eyes

Born on December 2, 1981, Britney Jean Spears came into this world with a twink-twink-twinkle in her eye — a star from the start. Her mom, Lynne, says, "Even as a little baby, Britney was a real darling . . . she has always been noticed." Dad Jamie, a building contractor, agrees.

Britney may not have done somersaults out of her crib, but as soon as she could walk she began tapping that Britney beat. She claims that she was bopping as early as age two. Mom Lynne confirms it — and Mom would know! She's been at Britney's side through thick and thin.

From the very beginning, both of Britney's parents encouraged her energy and talent one hundred percent, enrolling her in a variety of dancing and gymnastics classes. Every day Britney and her mom would drive to gymnastics classes an hour south of Kentwood — to Covington, Louisiana.

In classes, the floor exercise and the uneven parallel bars were Britney's best (and favorite) gymnastic events. She practiced up to three hours each day. But after a while Britney got discouraged. She wasn't as strong as some other girls. She fell off the balance beam. She missed tumbling moves.

Britney decided that gymnastics wasn't what she really wanted. She realized that she would never be an Olympic medalist. Fortunately, she also realized that years of tumbling practice hadn't gone to waste. They helped to make her a super strong dancer. From that moment on, she set her sights on the dancing stage, performing in her first talent show when she was only six.

Three years later, by age nine, Britney was traveling around regularly to dance competitions. Her specialty: jazz lyrical dancing. Fans can see some jazzy steps in all of her music videos, no doubt inspired by those early experiences. Fans can also see traces of Britney's gymnastics roots. Believe it or not, in the . . . *Baby One More Time* video, that's Britney doing her own back flips.

With a Song in Her Heart

Of course, dancing is only a small piece of Britney's big talent. Singing is what really makes her smile. At the wee age of four, Britney sang a heartfelt rendition of "What Child Is This?" for her church's kindergarten graduation. Unsurprisingly, she was a smash success. Every now and then Britney pulls out the videotape of that momentous "first" concert appearance and watches it just for fun. She laughs when she sees herself. "I kept tilting my head to the side, I was so nervous!"

Britney remembers the exact moment in time when she realized that she could be a singer — for real. She was bouncing on a trampoline in her Louisiana backyard, singing at the top of her lungs, when her mom suddenly "heard" her for the first time. "My mom said to me, 'You can really *sing!*' and then she dragged me inside the house to sing some more." At that moment, mother and daughter saw the handwriting on the wall: Britney Spears was a singing star waiting to happen. Anything was possible.

That afternoon, Mom enrolled Britney in singing lessons and encouraged her daughter to do even more performing. Britney remembers her mom's single-minded commitment to Britney's singing ambition. "She would have company over when I was little, and she got so used to me [singing], she didn't even realize I was doing it all the time. And the company was always like, 'Lynne, tell her to be quiet.'" Mom didn't listen to the guests. Britney never got quiet. They had bigger plans.

Over the years Britney won numerous pageants and talent competitions that combined her dancing and singing talents. She won first place in the Kentwood Dairy Festival when she was only five. A display case in the Spearses' house is jam-packed with trophies and other awards from those days. At age seven, Britney won a silver first-prize trophy for Miss Talent USA, held in Monroe, Louisiana. The trophy is 58 inches — taller than Britney was at the time when she won it!

Britney was also a big MTV fan when she was younger. Her brother, Bryan (who's a few years older than Britney), says that his sister used to dance and sing in front of the television. What was she watching? Madonna videos!

Britney agrees. "At an early age, I'd scream it out!" She'd sing into a hairbrush, hairspray bottle, spoon, or anything she could find to serve as a makeshift microphone. It was karaoke night every night at the Spearses' house. Britney had a whole lotta love for dancing . . . singing . . . and much more. It was only the beginning.

CHAPTER 2
Family Girl

"My family has always supported me
one hundred percent."
[*Entertainment Weekly*]

Britney got her awesome go-getter attitude and rock-solid confidence from her mom. However, Lynne Spears, a second-grade teacher, didn't drive an unwilling Britney into the spotlight. Nothing could be further from the truth.

Britney assured one interviewer, "I didn't get into show business because I've got a pushy mother. She's not one of those stage moms. It was always me who wanted to do all of the performing." Lynne has always been there to support her daughter's desires because she trusts Britney. Her mom's support and encouragement have been the one constant in this young pop star's busy life.

"Mom was always saying 'Go for what you want,'" Britney says proudly. "I love [her] more than anything. It's great to have such a supportive person in my life. She's my best friend." No matter what's happening with the music, the touring, or the stardom — home (with mom) is where Britney's heart is.

When Britney is on the road, she misses her mother more than anything. She tries calling home every day. "Thank God for cellular phones!" Britney declares. "I am always on the phone 24/7."

Life on the road can be tough stuff. Believe it or not, even Britney Spears, America's teen queen, gets bummed out and homesick sometimes. After hours of traveling and performing in a new city every night, Britney confessed in an on-line chat that sometimes she heads back to her hotel room and just curls up to sleep . . . thinking of Kentwood. "You go into the hotel and you have grilled cheeses — but they're not like your momma's."

But there is always a light at the end of the tunnel. Britney's never sad for long once Momma Spears gets her baby girl back on track with a positive word of encouragement and a friendly reminder that, at the end of the day, family is what counts. That's when Britney books a flight home. She admits she needs a regular family fix in order to keep functioning.

Every six weeks Britney tries to make an official Kentwood pit stop. "My record label is really cool about letting me go home whenever I need a break, so I do get to spend time with my family," Britney explains. She dashes home for hugs, homemade cooking, and quality "hanging out" time with her mom, dad, older brother Bryan, baby sister Jamie-Lynn, and the family rottweiler Kane.

Send in the Sibs!

Britney calls brother Bryan, who's twenty-two, her guardian angel. "He's like the protective older brother, you know, always making sure I'm all right." Bryan is like ordinary country college boys. "He's into football and stuff like that," she adds. Actually, he is a college student studying kinesiology (the way the human body moves). Although they don't get to spend that much time together, sometimes bro and sis will shoot hoops in the driveway. Britney used to play basketball at Parklane Academy, the private local high school they both attended.

Baby sister Jamie-Lynn, on the other hand, is Britney's "partner in crime"! Just like her big sis, nine-year-old Jamie-Lynn (named for her mother and father) loves to sing. Britney often wonders if J-L will fill her pop star shoes at some point in the future. Britney told one interviewer, "[Jamie-

Lynn] is such a little spitfire there's no telling what she'll do."

No trip home to Louisiana is complete without a girls-only night with Jamie-Lynn and Britney's mom. The three of them pile up cushy pillows in the middle of the living room floor and cozy down to watch movies. In the Spearses' house, anytime is the right time for some major girl-bonding over A+ rentals like *Steel Magnolias* or *Titanic,* two of Britney's favorite flicks. Jamie-Lynn always insists on being in the middle so she can snuggle with her big sister — and role model — Britney Jean.

In May 2000, Lynne and Britney released a book they wrote together called *Britney Spears Heart to Heart.* The pair describes the transition from Britney's childhood experiences growing up in Kentwood to making it big as a musical superstar. Britney worked on a book with "Mom" because their relationship is so important to her. She told *USA Today*, "I always have her to confide in. I think that's really important. There are a lot of my friends who never talk to their moms about anything. They have nobody to go to except their friends. If they're in the wrong crowd, who can they call when they're in trouble?"

Britney wants her book to show how important

communication is between friends and between parents and children. "I've had my times when I've gone out and partied. I know what it's like. It's because they're lacking something in their life — maybe the feeling of being loved. . . . Parents and teenagers don't have the quality time they used to."

Hello! Good-bye!

The worst part about coming home to Kentwood, Louisiana . . . is leaving again. "As usual, Britney and I get teary-eyed every time we have to part," Lynne writes to fans on Britney's official Web site. "We try to talk about when we'll be together again." Britney concedes that good-bye is her least favorite word.

But good-byes are nothing new to the Spears clan. Britney and her mom have grown accustomed to saying hello in one breath and good-bye in the next. Since the start of her career, Britney's been on the road nonstop. But she still manages to find time for her family.

CHAPTER 3

From NYC to MMC

*"Onstage, I'm the happiest person
in the world."*

[*People* magazine]

When Britney was nine, in the midst of her dance performances and talent pageants, she learned about an audition for the television show *The New Mickey Mouse Club* (*MMC*), a remake of an old TV show from the 1950s. The audition was being held in Atlanta, Georgia. Britney knew she had to try out for it. Mom and Dad weren't necessarily convinced. Atlanta was a long drive from Kentwood. But, as usual, Lynne and her husband, Jamie, supported Britney's dreams. They traveled to the tryout anyway.

Britney was up against more than 600 other kids for a spot on the new show — but the pressure never got to her. She aced her auditions. Britney made it through several rounds of cuts and ended up as one of seven finalists.

But she didn't get the part. Unfortunately, the

show's producers thought Britney was too young for *MMC*'s TV cast at the time. Britney was heartbroken. But then, something amazing happened. Those same producers went out of their way to tell Britney and her family how impressed they were with her talent. They suggested that perhaps — when Britney got a little bit older — that she might return for another audition. They then suggested she travel to New York City to get an agent and get some hands-on stage-and-film experience.

When Britney's mom and dad heard this, they were enthusiastic. So was Britney! What next? New York City, of course. They would follow the advice of the *MMC* casting team. Britney and her mom moved to New York right away to see what they could do. That's when they started working with high-powered entertainment lawyer Larry Rudolph — who taught the two all about being in show biz. Meanwhile, Dad stayed back in Kentwood with Bryan and Jamie-Lynn, who had to stay in school.

Give My Regards to Broadway

New York City was a blur of "Lights, camera, and action!" for ten-year-old Britney, yet she adjusted quickly to the pace and the people. "New

York's energy grows on you," she revealed. When she first got there, she attended the Professional Performing Arts School and off-Broadway Dance Center. She took classes for the next three years.

As she had hoped, her professional career quickly got in gear. She starred in a few commercials for products like BBQ sauce and Mitsubishi cars. But mostly she auditioned, acted, and sang her way through the Big Apple . . . until 1991, when she got her first big break.

That's when Britney was cast in the leading role in an off-Broadway comedy called *Ruthless*. She had been the understudy — but ended up playing the lead. In the show, Britney played a bratty kid gone bad. Since it was a musical, Britney had a perfect opportunity to show off her singing, dancing, and acting skills at the same time.

In one interview, Britney said what she loved best about doing *Ruthless* was being able to play a character who is both naughty and nice. Although she found performing the same show day after day exhausting and sometimes even a little tiresome, acting in *Ruthless* was a life-changing experience. Once Britney stepped onto that stage, she had a taste of the city spotlight.

There was no turning back now.

Time for TV

After she left *Ruthless* in 1992, Britney headed home again for a traditional Louisiana Christmas. She missed her family and friends. Lynne and Jamie put the almost eleven-year-old Britney back in school for a few months. She tried to adjust, but she missed show business too much. She wanted to get out and audition again. Britney needed to be singing and dancing — or she just didn't feel like herself.

That summer, Britney and her mom heard about an open call for the hot television show *Star Search*. On the show, kids and adults competed in different categories like "Best Kid Singer" or "Best Spokesmodel." Britney's mom loaded up the car and off they went to the audition, just an hour away in Baton Rouge, the capital city of Louisiana.

Once again, just like at her *MMC* audition, Britney impressed casting directors. This time, however, they wanted her . . . and they wanted her right away! Britney was invited to fly to Los Angeles to perform on *Star Search* in front of millions of television viewers. Amazingly, once on the show, Britney won her first round of competition. She was ecstatic! Unfortunately, when she came back the next week to compete against another contestant, she lost.

But Britney didn't let that setback slow her down. She had made it to television for the very first time. Now she knew she was ready for bigger, better things. It was time to give *The New Mickey Mouse Club* another try.

Getting Her Ears

Things had been going her way . . . but now Britney Jean Spears was about to have her greatest stroke of good fortune. She booked a special audition back at Disney, and tried out for *MMC,* baby — one more time!

Luckily for Britney, one more time was all she needed. Although this time she faced more than fifteen thousand auditionees who tried out in thirteen major cities in the United States and Canada, Britney felt more confident than ever before. After a lengthy three-day screen test, she was selected as one of the seven new Mouseketeers.

At long last, she'd earned her Mickey Mouse ears! How did she feel — after all this time? "It was like a dream come true. It was all I'd really wanted since I was eight. They called on the phone and said 'You're going to be a Mouseketeer' and I just started screaming." After that, she moved with Mom — and

Jamie-Lynn, too, this time — to Orlando, Florida, where the show was taped. Once again, her family supported her success, her decisions, and her "real-life" star search.

Mousing Around

The newest *MMC* cast had to rap, sing, dance, and act in as many as fifty-five episodes each year — and Britney was on the show for two years (from 1992 to 1994). How did she manage to make it through more than one hundred and ten skits and songs? No problem! Once again, Britney was getting the best possible training for her future career as a singer. "When I was on *MMC* I learned that I had a major love of music."

Other Mouseketeers at that time were a few other now-famous faces (and voices) like Keri Russell (from *Felicity*), J.C. Chasez and Justin Timberlake (from 'N Sync), and Christina Aguilera. The whole group worked together like a family!

The schedule was not easy, however. Britney and the others were juggling *MMC* with their on-set schooling. The cast got up early — just after seven in the morning. From nine to noon, they had school lessons and then they went off to show rehearsals.

Finally, at four o'clock, the show taped until seven at night. Immediately following, the Mouseketeers went back home to eat, do homework, and go to sleep. This cycle continued every day through the end of the season.

But Britney loved every minute — even the hard ones. If you ask Britney what was the coolest part of the *MMC* job, she answers with no hesitation: everything. The schedule was difficult, but it had so many things going for it.

It was cool because it introduced her to people who could help take her career to the next level. It was cool because she learned so much from the show's cast and directors. Most of all, it was cool because Mouseketeers got special perks! The cast reported to work on the MGM studios lot, which was located next door to the Magic Kingdom, so Britney, J.C., Justin, Christina, and the others could go on rides during breaks. Some job! Britney says Space Mountain and Rockin' Roller Coaster are her favorites.

Unhappily, in 1994, *MMC* was canceled. The ride was over. What were Britney and the rest of the Mouseketeers supposed to do now?

CHAPTER 4
Jive Talkin'

"I would rather perform than do anything."
[*USA Today*]

After the plug was pulled on *MMC*, Britney headed back to Louisiana and put her stardom on temporary hold to return to her hometown school, Parklane Academy, for junior year. Britney had no singing or dancing offers on the table. She figured that extra time off from performing would make her appreciate her family, friends, and hometown that much more. And it did — sort of.

At age fifteen, Britney was starting to live the life of a "normal" teenager again. Sometimes kids would come up to her and say, "Hey, I saw you on *The Mickey Mouse Club!*" but mostly they kept to themselves. "I did the homecoming thing and the prom thing," she recalls. She mused to *Girls' Life* magazine, "Everyone really knew me before, so it wasn't like anyone was putting on an act around me.

My friends and I still acted stupid around each other, like always."

But, Britney was getting itchier by the moment. She needed to get out and perform onstage. Britney missed that spotlight. "I need to sing and I love to travel."

So Britney Jean left Parklane and started "Jive" talkin'.

Once again, her parents were there to support her. She had recorded several songs on a home-made demo (short for "demonstration") tape. She picked songs that would showcase her range of talent. Her dad, Jamie, called Larry Rudolph, who had represented Britney years before, and asked him for his help. Could he get Britney another job in New York? Larry responded by putting Britney's demo tape into the hands of a top executive at Jive Records. Jive was already responsible for such artists as the Backstreet Boys, 'N Sync, and R. Kelly.

From the moment Jeff Fenster, senior vp of artists and recording, heard Britney's beautiful voice, he knew he'd found something special. Jeff later told the press, "She was intriguing, so we had her come in and audition for us in person." Meetings like that almost never happen — but Britney got her shot. She knew she had to make the most of it.

Britney's live audition songs? "Jesus Loves Me" and Whitney Houston's "I Have Nothing."

Britney's nerves? Frazzled.

Britney's chances of getting a record deal? One in a million.

Audition Day

Mom and daughter went to the Jive Records audition together, fingers and toes crossed. Would this be the next big break Britney needed?

While Britney was belting out her two songs, her mother nervously mouthed the words. Lynne Spears wanted this record deal for her daughter more than anything else. Britney later told reporters, "I felt a little weird standing in a conference room, basically singing for my life . . . but it's rough out there. You have to take whatever opportunities come your way and make the most of them."

She told *J-14* magazine, "It was sort of nerve-racking. I went in there and there were, like, these ten executive people sitting there just staring at me.

I was like, 'Oh my goodness, I'm just going to close my eyes and do the best that I can do.'"

The best she could do did the trick. She was the right talent in the right place at the right time. Jeff Fenster was floored.

"It's very rare that we sign someone on the spot," he admitted later to the magazine *Hit Sensations*, "but once we heard [Britney] sing in our office, we offered her a deal right there." Jive's next step? They would send Britney into the studio to make her first record.

Everything was falling into place.

CHAPTER 5

Oh Bay-Bay, Bay-Bay: The First Album

"My wildest dream? What I'm experiencing right now . . . making the album."

[MTV Online]

Britney Spears packed her bags. Jive was sending her places! The company arranged for her to work with Max Martin, who produces songs for the Backstreet Boys and other stars, and Eric Foster White, who has produced the diva Whitney Houston and others. Britney'd be working and recording in two locations, but when they were through she'd have one awesome album.

For a sixteen-year-old girl from Kentwood, Louisiana, going into the recording studio was like entering a whole new world! Of course she loved every minute of it. Those few whirlwind weeks cutting the eleven tracks off her freshman CD, . . . *Baby One More Time*, changed her life. ("Cutting" a track is when you record it onto tape and then mix it with background vocals and music.) Britney was doing what she loved! Her dreams really were coming true.

First stop: Sweden.

Max's studio was located where he lives, in the European country of Sweden. Britney would be going overseas for the very first time! She could hardly contain her excitement. "When I signed, I was like, 'This is too good to be true!'"

Britney and Max worked long hours together at Sweden's prestigious Cherion Studios, where 'N Sync, the Backstreet Boys, and Ace of Base had all recorded their hip music. Britney's sound was coming along perfectly. In one interview Max said, "She's got a good sense of catching the melody, performing it, and taking it to the next level."

Together, Britney and Max set down six tracks in no time! They were having too much fun, Britney thought to herself. She sensed that this album would have a hit. Britney could feel it from the top of her head to the tips of her toes.

Second stop: New Jersey.

When Max finished up, Britney came back to the United States and went into a studio in New Jersey with Eric Foster White to finish the remaining five songs on the record. Again things went very well with the team of musicians and producers. "It was a case of good chemistry among a group of very talented people," Eric told *Billboard* magazine.

Although Britney did not write most of the songs herself, she was involved with the creation of the music and the lyrics on all of the CD's tracks. She knew what she wanted her album to be like from the very beginning, telling Max and Eric, "I don't want to go over the top." What Britney wanted to do was go *right* to the top instead.

When the album came out of production, Britney's management and Jive Records started an unprecedented marketing campaign to launch their newest artist. They wanted to capture a teen audience for Britney as quickly as they could.

First, the team at Jive Records created a 1-800 toll-free number so kids could dial in and hear free music samples from Britney. Then, Jive set up a World Wide Web page with behind-the-scenes articles about how Britney got started and how she was enjoying her musical career. Finally, in mid-1998, many months before the first album was set to release, Jive sent out thousands of postcards to teen magazine subscribers. Inside copies of *Seventeen* and other publications, a Britney postcard smiled back at fans as if to say, "You may not know me right now . . . but you WILL!"

It's a Mall World After All, Y'all

Three months before the "official" release of . . . *Baby One More Time,* Jive sent Britney packing . . . on a mini-tour! She embarked on a singing junket to different shopping malls across the United States. Jive wanted to put Britney smack-dab in the middle of her potential fans. Britney admitted to *People* magazine that, "No one knew who I was, but I could see that they really enjoyed my music." At the mall events, Britney helped to hand out "Britney Packs" jammed with lip gloss, CD-samplers, and more. She toured thirty-seven cities in only twenty-one days.

There was definitely no jive about Jive Record's wishes for this singer's immediate future. When the execs at Jive learned that the mall tour was paying off . . . there was a buzz in the air about the next big thing. Britney Spears was the next big thing.

Britney couldn't believe they were talking about her.

The Kentwood teen's natural, sweet self won her an immediate audience with kids and adults alike. Teen fans liked the way Britney moved and sang. Girls wanted to be like her, while boys wanted to be with her. Parents liked Britney's self-confidence and energy. Her energetic public appearances — shaking hands and meeting with top managers and radio programmers across the country, and conducting numerous on-air interviews — made an indelible impression on everyone involved in the prelaunch and launch of her first record.

Jive Records continued to promote the hot new singer as often as they could, in as many creative ways as possible. She was a guest singer on Sunglass Hut's preholiday CD in 1998 . . . she posed for the cover of *just nikki* :) girls' catalog and *'zine* . . . and she even made a guest appearance with the ever-popular Backstreet Boys on Hasbro's Girl Talk CD-ROM software.

In the meantime, Britney was bracing herself for success. What do you think it feels like to know that your dream is one step closer to coming true?

Britney Gets 'N Sync

One day Britney got some more wonderful news. She was chosen to be an opening act for a part of the 1998 'N Sync tour. This was her biggest break yet. 'N Sync were burning up the charts with "Tearin' Up My Heart," and their live appearances were sold out nationwide. Once Britney joined their tour, she would be seen by millions of potential new fans.

Britney states that it was hard opening for 'N Sync because she didn't know what to expect from the audience. She told MTV Networks that at first she was intimidated by the mostly female crowds. "Oh, my God, you should see these screaming girls. It's unreal . . . I mean, the things they do . . . It's sooo bizarre!" In fact, Britney always feared the worst possible reaction to her performance. She knew that word had gotten out that a girl was opening up for the hot boy band. She expected to hear fans screeching, "Who are you?" "Get off the stage!" and "GO AWAY!"

Luckily, she guessed wrong. The negative reactions were all inside her head. In the real world, the response to Britney's mall performances and 'N Sync sets was nothing but stellar. After Britney started to sing and dance, the fans started to squeal! They liked her . . . they really liked her! It probably didn't hurt that Brit had guy dancers up there with her, too. She wasn't completely alone up there.

Shortly after Britney's part of the 'N Sync tour

was happening, Jive Records officially released the first single, off ... *Baby One More Time* for radio play. Britney's beautiful voice hit the airwaves at last! Britney remembers the exact moment when she heard the title track ". . . Baby One More Time." "I was returning home . . . I had just gotten off the airplane and I got in the car. . . . We'd gotten all the luggage and heard it on the car radio. It came on and it was weird . . . soooo weird. We'd accomplished so much up to that point."

The team at Jive Records wanted absolutely everyone to know Britney Spears. Soon enough, everyone would.

Toppin' the Pop Charts

Jive released the single " . . . Baby One More Time" at the end of December 1998. In January 1999, it climbed — *boom!* — into the number-one position on the *Billboard* charts. Previously an unknown pop performer, Britney Spears suddenly found herself at the top of the pop heap! Only a few weeks after her seventeenth birthday, Britney saw all of her hard work paying off. This was the *best* birthday present ever!

Jive released the album . . . *Baby One More*

Time on January 12, 1999. It took less than a week to make its mark. On January 18, 1999, Britney's manager called to share the unbelievable news! "Are you sitting down?" he asked her. She almost fainted. Her album debuted in the top slot. Meanwhile, her single was still up on top, too.

That meant that her single and her album were number one at the same time. This was the first and only time a new female artist had done this. Not only that, but she was also the youngest artist ever to debut with a single and an album at number one since the duo Kris Kross did it in 1992.

Britney freaked out. She had a one-two chart punch! She was a star! Kids across the country were singing her song! She was breaking music records!

Can you imagine what that must have felt like? Britney was making history.

CHAPTER 6

Hittin' the Road

"When I am out on the road I don't have time to do anything . . . I don't have time to get in any trouble."

[MTV Online]

In early 1999, Britney was careful not to fall out of sync with 'N Sync. After two months with "the boys," she was starting to do her own star-girl thing, and she was busier than ever. She was getting up at the crack of dawn, rehearsing for her own midsummer concert dates, and practicing numbers for her second video shoot. . . .

And then there was that left knee.

In February 1999, Britney was injured during a video rehearsal for her second big hit song, "Sometimes." "I was kicking my right leg up and the left leg just collapsed," Britney explained to the teen magazines. Ouch! She went to the hospital one-two-three, where docs performed arthroscopic surgery to repair torn cartilage in her knee.

What a super-trooper! Britney was only out of surgery for four days when she managed to help co-host the kickoff party for MTV's spring break cruise along the New Orleans riverfront. After that, she hopped around on crutches for three whole weeks. She ended up missing an appearance on *The Tonight Show with Jay Leno,* but Britney knew she'd get her chance to appear again. She was more concerned with getting better.

Amazingly, the freaky knee incident turned out to be for the best. Britney had been going full-steam ahead since getting the Jive Records deal and the 'N Sync tour. Her injury meant she could cool it in Kentwood for a few weeks.

By the middle of the summer, Britney's knee was way better. Now it was time for her to fly solo — headlining her own tour event. "Oh, Lordy, pop music for me, it just puts me in a good mood," she said. "Some people say [touring is] the most grueling part — going to London, Germany, Spain, Italy, or Canada — but I disagree. Promotion is the crazy part."

For Britney, concerts are the best.

Summer 1999

Starting on June 28, 1999, in Pompano, Florida, Britney Spears headlined her first fun tour with fellow teen artists C-Note, Third Storee, and Boyz and Girlz United. Their destination? Fifty cities across the United States and Canada. The tour was scheduled from June through the fall. No sooner had Britney's knee healed, than she was on the road again. Her tour was generously sponsored by Tommy Hilfiger.

Was this Southern belle suddenly becoming . . . the Energizer Bunny? Since her first hit song, this Louisiana teen queen had been "seen" in a major way. She still showed no signs of slowing down.

As always, she was happy to hear that fans were pleased with her performances all over North America. "Crowds for my shows have all been really responsive. I've been lucky." Britney wanted to make sure she was always putting on the best show she could. Her fan base supported her, and she supported them right back with a kickin' hour-long set at each concert. Usually, Britney also plans a pre-concert meeting for special fans. Since she started headlining her own tours, Britney developed a tradition of "meeting and greeting" (translation: She hangs out, has a "soda pop," takes a few pics, and answers a few questions with a select group of local fans). Usually, the lucky guests are local fan club leaders and radio promotion winners.

Spring 2000

Still no signs of slowing down!

After touring for most of 1999, Britney moved into the new millennium without a hitch. As always, she was intent upon giving her fans what they want most of all: MORE BRITNEY! In the winter months, she stopped touring only briefly so that she could record her second album. And as soon as she was out of the studio — the tour schedule heated up once again.

In March 2000, she launched a U.S. tour as a "warm-up" (like she needed to get warm!) for the summer 2000 tour to support her second album. The "warm-up" tour gave Brit a chance to try out some of her newest tunes and dance moves on a live crowd — long before the album was in stores. True to the album title, *Oops! . . . I Did It Again,* Britney was out there onstage once again, doin' it: dancing, jumping, tumbling, and singing her heart out for a crowd of very fortunate fans. Starting March 8 and ending on April 8, the "warm-up" lasted for one month — exactly.

Just after her tour started (in late March), a busy Britney took a three-day detour into Universal Studios, where she filmed the first video for *Oops!. . . I Did It Again*. Britney's fast-paced schedule gave her a burst of energy for the out-of-this-world video shoot, set on another planet. Unfortunately, Britney had a bout of bad luck when a camera bopped this princess of pop right on the top of her head. Britney, however, was unfazed by the accident. She wrapped up production the next day!

Spring Break? Study Break!

In the middle of the touring and video-making mayhem, Britney stopped off to share in the festivities with MTV Spring Break 2000 in Cancún with stars like Destiny's Child, Enrique Iglesias, and Jay-Z. Believe it or not, after soaking up some sun and dancing on the beach . . . Britney hit the books!

When she has downtime, Britney likes to keep up with school stuff. It's a tough task, being on the road so much and still trying to get homework done, but she knows how important it is to study. Since she's unable to make it back to her hometown school, Parklane, for regular classes, Britney has found other ways to get smart . . . on the go! In addition to studying with tutors, Britney enrolled for correspondence classes through the University of Nebraska.

Still working on her degree through 2000, Britney hopes to get her high school diploma soon. Then will Britney apply to colleges? Britney says she'd love to study entertainment law someday.

But first, the tour must go on. . . .

Summer 2000

Ta-da!

After so much anticipation, the *Oops! . . . I Did It Again* world tour officially kicked off in June 2000, with a hot opening act: A*Teens.

Britney is readier than ever to show the fans another side of her they have not seen before. She says that she's modeling her approach on one of her idols, Madonna. Like Madonna, Brit wants to create a new look and persona for each new project she works on. For two months Britney's been bouncing around different U.S. locations and after this summer — she'll go global.

This fall, Britney will tour overseas for the

very first time — making the "world" part of the
world tour official. She spoke to MTV about her
plans: "I'm going to go to Europe, and just basically
go everywhere for six months, so I'm really excited
about that because I've never toured outside of the
United States. I've never experienced other fans in
other places. Performing in front of them is going to
be so exciting."

Is it your turn to catch this cutie in concert?
Britney may be on her way to your town now, so
make a note of these upcoming *Oops!* dates and
places. See you there. . . .

August 2000

08/01/00	Concord, CA	Concord Pavilion
08/03/00	San Diego, CA	San Diego Sports Arena
08/04/00	Las Vegas, NV	MGM Grand
08/06/00	Sacramento, CA	Sacramento Valley Amphitheatre
08/08/00	Mountain View, CA	Shoreline Amphitheatre
08/10/00	Portland, OR	Rose Garden Arena
08/11/00	Seattle, WA	The Gorg
08/14/00	Salt Lake City, UT	Delta Center
08/21/00	Pittsburgh, PA	Star Lake Amphitheatre
08/28/00	Boston, MA	Tweeter Center

08/30/00	Saratoga, NY	SPAC
08/31/00	Cleveland, OH	Gund Arena

September 2000

09/01/00	Cincinnati, OH	Riverbed Amphitheatre
09/02/00	Indianapolis, IN	Deer Creek
09/03/00	Columbus, OH	Polaris Amphitheatre
09/05/00	Nashville, TN	First American Music Center
09/06/00	Atlanta, GA	Lakewood Amphitheatre
09/09/00	Orlando, FL	Orlando Arena
09/10/00	West Palm Beach	Coral Sky Amphitheatre

CHAPTER 7
Oops! The Second Album

*"People assume I'm some puppet and people are
telling me what to do all the time. When I first got
signed to a record label, I was fifteen. So I did have
some help at first. . . . But now, with experience
and as time goes on, I know what I need."*

(*USA Today*)

Oops! She did it once — she's doing it twice!
Last winter in 1999, Britney went back to Europe
for a series of intense studio sessions in Sweden and
Switzerland with her old friends, producers Max
Martin, Eric Foster White, and others. She had the
opportunity to work with some new composers like
her favorite Diane Warren, Robert "Mutt" Lange
(he's married to Shania Twain), and superstar producer Babyface.

The first single, the title track "Oops! . . . I Did
It Again" hit radio airwaves in April 2000, while the
album itself was released in May. Her video for

"Oops!" hit number one on MTV's *TRL*, thanks to viewers' votes. Destined straight for the top again? Of course!

Her sound changed a little for the new album — and she's excited to share that with her fans! "My material is a little more mature-sounding. My voice has really matured more and I think it will probably have a little more hip-hop flair." As fans would expect, Britney wanted to try something that challenged her. Who doesn't? Britney is a risk-taker — and after two years at the top, she's developed a savvy sense about where she wants to see herself musically and personally.

She told MTV, "I've grown as an artist. Generally, [the new album *Oops! . . . I Did It Again* is] still pop music, but I think it's a little bit funkier. It's more 'now,' the music's now. It's really funky."

What makes it funky? For one thing, Britney covers the classic "(I Can't Get No) Satisfaction" by the Rolling Stones. She told *USA Today*, "I was just like, I like this song and I think it will be a really cool combination working with [hip-hop producer] Rodney [Jerkins — who's worked with Brandy and Monica] and doing a really funky song." Jerkins agrees wholeheartedly. "I'm gonna give her a more . . .

Janet Jackson feel." With that kind of "attitude," this album will produce some first-rate, funky videos, too. Look to that *TRL* countdown — no doubt Britney will be spending a good part of the fall in heavy MTV video rotation.

Perhaps the best thing about the new *Oops!* album is the fact that Britney worked on many of the songs herself. She shares some of the writing credit on the CD's liner notes. Over the last year, she put a lot of time and thought into making that happen. Even when she was out on the road, she was trying to stay focused on what her new music could be. "[I was] always calling my answering machine and leaving messages with lyrics for songs."

One of the dreamiest songs on *Oops!* is called "Dear Diary," which Britney wrote herself. She says it is "about a girl who is interested in this guy and she comes home every night and writes about it." Not really pop or funk, but somewhere in between . . . this tune sounds like a guaranteed hit. She confided to MTV, "It's a really sweet song about a girl's innermost thoughts, and what she's feeling inside. You know, you're writing to your journal or your diary (which I do, so I can totally relate to it) and it comes from the heart, so it's special."

Are fans really surprised to hear another romantic love song smash from the pop princess?

Not when you're talking about Britney.

These days music is the "love" of Britney's life.

CHAPTER 8

She Wants It ALL!

"I think it boils down to talent, and believing in yourself, and having people around you believing, as well."

(MTV Online)

She sings. She dances. She acts? She wishes! Unfortunately, Britney finds little free time in between her endless touring and record-making to shoot anything more than those music videos. She explained to *Teen People,* "There are, like, twenty scripts waiting for me, but I haven't taken them seriously because I know I don't have the time!"

Of course, there are exceptions to every rule. Britney hasn't completely ignored her acting bug.

Sabrina, the Teenage Witch

In fall 1999, Britney took a brief break to join best buddy Melissa Joan Hart on the set of her hit show *Sabrina, the Teenage Witch.* It was a small screen cameo and Britney played . . . who else? Britney! Here's how the whole thing happened:

1. Melissa was starring in a brand-new movie that sounded like it had hit written all over it . . . but no one could agree on the right title.
2. The folks who were working on the movie's sound track got an idea. They loved Britney's song "(You Drive Me) Crazy." In no time, the movie execs decided that was the best name for the flick: *Drive Me Crazy.*
3. In order to promote the movie and the song, managers and producers came up with one wild idea: put Melissa in Britney's *Crazy* video — and give Britney a cool cameo on Melissa's hit show *Sabrina, the Teenage Witch.*

That's exactly what happened. (P.S. You'll also find a Brit hit on another Melissa-related album. "Soda Pop" can be heard on *Sabrina*'s TV soundtrack.)

The Truth About *Dawson's Creek*

Also in 1999, Columbia TriStar TV announced that it was considering Britney for a role in her own show or project. The studio sent out press releases and other notices to create interest and excitement. The studio, which handles the WB's *Dawson's Creek*, also claimed Brit's first "big" role was supposed to have been a guest-starring spot on last season's *Dawson's Creek*. Ha-ha — they said she'd play a geek in the show. Soon enough fans everywhere were crossin' their fingers hoping that sparks might fly sometime soon between Brit and one of the WB hunks like James Van Der Beek. In an interview, Brit admitted that she's a *Dawson* kinda girl, telling *Twist* magazine that she "met him on New Year's Eve in Las Vegas and he's very nice." Unfortunately, Britney never shot the episode as planned — she was just too busy touring!

Big Screen Cameos — and Beyond

She did make one big screen cameo so far in a movie that was filmed last summer in 1999. Fans will have a chance to see her in the release of *Jack of All Trades,* a film produced by Trans Continental

Records, the same company that helped groups like the Backstreet Boys and 'N Sync get started. Super-groups like Take 5, LFO, C-Note, and others will also have cameos in the flick. Look for a bubbly Brit as a flight attendant, delivering hot coffee to two pilots played by country singer Kenny Rogers and Harry Casey from KC and the Sunshine Band.

For now, acting plans take a backseat to her music. She continues to get TV and film offers, but she's focused on making *Oops! . . . I Did It Again* an even bigger success than . . . *Baby One More Time*. Britney revealed, "I have a management team in L.A. They hook up with films and everything, and I really would like to do a film just to experience something a little different, but I am so focused on my music right now!"

Someday Brit will probably star in a movie — but it'll probably be the saga of her own "crazy" life. Of course, for the *Untitled Britney Jean Spears Movie,* casting directors would definitely have to track down 'N Sync or 98° — to play extras — right? And, of course, then there's Ben Affleck, her superduper crush of all time. He would be Britney's leading man, naturally. There's no chance Britney would turn that one down.

And the Beat Goes On . . .

Britney may not have time to star in her own TV show yet, but just when it seems like she's can't get any busier — she does! In spite of her music commitments, Britney makes time for activities besides music. She signed some unbelievable deals and endorsements during 1999–2000. Here are a few of the biggies Britney worked on:

- She launched the coolest Brit collectibles — also known as Britney Spears dolls! Each one is a twelve-inch plastic plaything with Brit's barely-there belly and blond locks! Britney appeared live on *The Rosie O'Donnell Show* to launch her pop star playthings, and to explain how the in-concert dolls came to be. Each one has a different 'do and comes with a platinum or gold CD single. One funny fact about the dolls: Britney's sis plays with them at home in Louisiana.
- "Chew" won't believe this — but Britney's got her own gum! Starting in 2000, she hooked up for a three-year relationship with Famous Fixins, a candy-and-

novelty-products company. They've been making a bunch of sweet stuff based on Brit, like CD-shaped bubble gum in a jewel case.

- Clairol signed on the teenage singing sensation to pitch their Herbal Essences line. Britney was chosen as a spokeswoman for the brand and immediately started appearing in television, print, and radio ads in spring of 2000.

For a Good Cause

Life isn't all bubble gum for Britney. She wants more than anything to make charity count for something as she builds her career.

In addition to giving a portion of all her profits away to The Giving Back Fund, Britney continues to make donations to causes she believes in. She also offers her time whenever necessary — to perform or attend important events for Nickelodeon's The Big Help and others.

Perhaps her most valuable charitable contribution has been the startup of her own foundation. Britney has started a performing arts camp for underprivileged kids that opened this summer. The camp is located in western Massachusetts — in the Berkshire Mountains, far away from the heat and beat of the city. The plan: Each summer Britney will give one hundred kids two weeks of summer workshops.

Brit told *Bop* magazine in an exclusive interview: "I just know there are so many young, talented people out there that aren't given the opportunity to express themselves creatively. And that's where I come in with this camp. . . . I'm going to have the best of vocal coaches, dance coaches, and choreographers. . . .

"My mom and I have been talking about the charity for some time. I've been so blessed, it's the right time to give back."

Britney told *Rolling Stone* magazine that she always considered her responsibility as a performer to "be a good example for kids out there." But she is also honest about the fact that she doesn't want to be a "serious" role model — preaching at fans and acting like she knows better than everyone else.

Instead, she lives her life in a positive, upbeat, and generous way, giving what she can, when she can . . . and encouraging her fans to do the same. By doing good, positive stuff, Britney knows she can be the smartest kind of role model for young kids and older teens.

CHAPTER 9
Listen Up! Discography

Albums:

. . . *Baby One More Time*
1. . . . Baby One More Time
2. (You Drive Me) Crazy
3. Sometimes
4. Soda Pop
5. Born to Make You Happy
6. From the Bottom of My Broken Heart
7. I Will Be There
8. I Will Still Love You (Duet with Don Philip)
9. Thinkin' About You
10. E-Mail My Heart
11. The Beat Goes On

Oops! . . . I Did It Again
1. Oops! . . . I Did It Again
2. Stronger

3. Don't Go Knockin' on My Door
4. Satisfaction (I Can't Get No)
5. Don't Let Me Be the Last to Know
6. What U See (Is What U Get)
7. Lucky
8. One Kiss from You
9. Where Are You Now
10. Can't Makc You Love Me
11. When Your Eyes Say It
12. Dear Diary

Singles:

(You Drive Me) Crazy
1. (You Drive Me) Crazy (The Stop Remix)
2. (You Drive Me) Crazy (The Stop Remix) (Instrumental)

Sometimes
1. Sometimes (Radio Edit)
2. I'm So Curious (The B-Side)
3. Sometimes (Soul Solution Mix)

Born to Make You Happy (Import)
1. Born to Make You Happy (Radio Edit)
2. Born to Make You Happy (Bonus Remix)
3. (You Drive Me) Crazy (Jazzy Jim's Hip-Hop Remix)
4. Born to Make You Happy (Answer Machine Message)

CHAPTER 10
Video Vault

When Britney was younger she said she'd "hang out in [her] room for hours watching Michael Jackson videos." Was she learning the moonwalk or some slick breakdancin' moves? Nope. But she was getting downright funky. You can see Michael's funk influence all over *(You Drive Me) Crazy* and the other Spears' videos. (Think: Michael's eighties vids like *Beat It* or maybe a more recent techno-beat like his duet with sister Janet, *Scream*). FYI: Britney has said many times that she thinks it would be hot to team up with Michael.

Madonna's influence is also obvious in Britney's videos. You can't deny Madonna's impact on a Brit-video like *Sometimes*. Does anyone see a little bit of *Cherish*? (Think: beach, lots of white clothes, love-

story theme.) Or maybe Madonna's early stuff —
Lucky Star or *Into the Groove*?

Brit doesn't need much to make her happy
when she's making a new video. As long as she's
dancing and playing and singing her southern heart
out — she's A-OK. About concert performances,
she told *Star Profile*, "I'll be the happiest person in
the world when I have . . . my dancers with me and
we just get out there and perform and kick butt!"
The same holds true for her videos.

In her vids, Britney does it all — from bubble
gum bebop to sugar-sweet soul. What are your favorites? Rate 'em and see if you can figure out the
stumpers, too!

. . . . *Baby One More Time*

Setting: Home sweet school. Actually, this is the
same high school where the 1970's flick *Grease* was
filmed — from the lockers to the gym.
Deep Meaning: Brit's broken up with a guy . . . but
now she regrets it and wants him back. Whoops!
Should have given that a little more thought, right?
Fashion Statements: Scene one: Schoolgirl/wild
child (FYI: It was Britney's idea to tie up her shirt
that way — not the director's); Scene two: Nice

pink tube top, Brit!; and Scene three: Gym gear is here, m'dear!

Hairy Stuff: Braids, ponytails on top of her head, pink bows

Dance Track: Funk and grind by the school lockers, in the school parking lot and gym — what more could you ask for?

Love Line: See that guy on the bleachers? He's the one! Should he take her back or not? P.S. In real life, the guy is Brit's cousin.

What You Didn't Know: Nigel Dick, the director of most of Britney's videos so far, said he wanted to make this debut video like a Power Rangers-style cartoon. Huh? Brit had 'em change it. She came up with the school idea. "I wanted something that teenagers could relate to." Can you imagine if they'd put Britney in a spangled, poofy jumpsuit instead of her schoolgirl getup? Could Brit really be "it" without that video's opening scene? Doubt it!

What Else You Didn't Know: The first time Britney saw this video on TV with friends from real life . . . everyone freaked out together! They were in a hotel room and they started jumping up and down on the bed and screaming! Also the "teacher" in the video is really Felicia Culotta, a family friend and Brit's chaperone when she's traveling.

Vid-stumpers! What time is it?

Just after 3 P.M.

Rate It! Any number from 1 to 10:
___Cool Factor
___ Brit's a BABE!
___ Hotties Here!
___ Love the Song
___Turn Off da Tube!

Sometimes

Setting: Meetcha down by Kenny's Cove on the pier, 'kay? (By the way: Kenny's Cove is named after one of the production scouts on the video. The actual setting was Paradise Cove, Malibu, California.)

Deep Meaning: Spot that beach boy! Brit spies her "love" roaming along the beach with his pooch. All the "beauty shots" in this one give it a hazy, glazy look — just like the look of love?

Fashion Statements: "Love at first sight" white as the color of choice; shimmering baby blue, too; and the softest, pinkest makeup the artist could find.

Hairy Stuff: Mousse madness? And Brit's not quite so blond in this one . . .

Dance Track: Getting down on the boardwalk . . .

soft but sweet. Her dancers look like they're having a good time anyway.

Love Line: Near the end of the video, Brit and her crew form the shape of . . . a HEART!

What You Didn't Know: Remember how Britney had knee surgery in spring 1999? Here's where it all happened. During one take, she kicked her right leg up and her left knee gave out. The video shoot had to be postponed. The video shoots for *Sometimes* started early . . . Brit had to be up and into hair and makeup by 5:30 A.M.

What Else You Didn't Know: Britney (not the director) got to choose the guy in the video — Chad — in a special casting session. (Heads up — there are no love stories here — Brit's strictly business when she works with guys.) And the dog was hand-picked, too! Her name is Hannah and she belongs to the video's producer.

Song Secret: On the b-side to the single of "Sometimes" you'll find the song "I'm So Curious." What's so secret about it? Britney really wrote it!

Vid-stumpers! What color is the beach ball Brit's holding when she dances on the pier?

Bright pink!

Candygirl: Britney "spears" her own brand
of bubble gum. It'll be CD-shaped.

Awardage: Britney took home the "Single of the Year" prize for ". . . Baby One More Time" at the first annual Teen Choice Awards.

Awardage, the sequel: She also snared the "Female Artist of the Year" award at the Billboard Music Awards in Las Vegas.

She's so e-*motion*-al! Britney's onstage moves are awesome. This was at the for charity Arthur Ashe Kids' Day at the U.S. Open.

A tender song requires a quiet concert moment. This one was for the ballad "From the Bottom of My Broken Heart."

Her onstage outfits — and her backup singers and dancers — are hyper slick.

Britney is "fashion-forward girl," in this sparkly formal gown she wore to the Billboard Music Awards.

She can also be "casual girl." The pig-tailed princess appeared at Nickelodeon's Big Help event and on behalf of her own charity, The Britney Spears Foundation.

Ultra Britney fans include actress Melissa Joan Hart, her *Drive Me Crazy* costar Mark Webber [left], singer/dancer Robbie Cerrico [right], plus the bands LFO, Lit, and *Boy Meets World*'s Danielle Fishel, who exclaims, "Britney is my favorite!"

Up the *Creek*? She was supposed to be in *Dawson's Creek*, but her schedule's been too crazy. James Van Der Beek is a friend, but Brit's favorite character on the show is Joey: "She's so cool."

Meeting and signing autographs for fans is a major perk of being a star.

Global-girl: This pic was snapped in the European country of Monaco. Brit's hits span the globe — she's charted in dozens of countries.

Gettin' wiggy wit' it: Well . . . every girl wants a change now and then.

Glam-girl: At the 2000 Grammy Awards, she looked every inch the mega star. Her performance won raves.

Britney's biggest fan: mom Lynne!

On her whirlwind cross-country tour, Brit did bits from her second album, *Oops! . . . I Did It Again*, as well as fan favorites from the first.

Pointing out the obvious:
Britney Spears is here to stay!

Rate It! Any number from 1 to 10:

___Cool Factor

___ Brit's a BABE!

___ Hotties Here!

___ Love the Song

___Turn Off da Tube!

(You Drive Me) Crazy

Setting: It's a postmodern nightclub gone . . . you guessed it . . . crazy! Britney said the set was "so exciting and so colorful and fun. It made things a lot more fun for me."

Deep Meaning: Britney says, "Me and my girlfriends are at this club and we're dorky waitresses. Then we see a cute guy and we decide we're gonna change — and get his attention . . . and so we change our clothes, our attitude, and start really dancing!"

Fashion Statements: Those cat's-eye glasses and that shiny, metallic green tube top!

Hairy Stuff: Ponytails and curlicues

Dance Track: Dance, jump, and rage on! Serious kicks. Techno-funky babes strut their stuff while basking in the neon glow of "CRAZY" in the background! Whew!

Love Line: When Britney says "My heart is jumping," we believe her! Everything's jumpin' in this techno-video!

What You Didn't Know: Well, you know this now — teen Sabrina Melissa Joan Hart has a cookin' cameo in this one! See page 47 for the whole scoop.

What Else You Didn't Know: This was definitely Britney's most expensive video yet! It was shot over a two-day period at Redondo Power Station in California.

Vid-stumpers! What special meeting did the director have to hold before the video started shooting? A safety meeting! This was a complicated set!

Rate It! Any number from 1 to 10:
___Cool Factor
___ Brit's a BABE!
___ Hotties Here!
___ Love the Song
___Turn Off da Tube!

From the Bottom of My Broken Heart (also known as FTBOMBH)

Setting: Technicolor lens shows this small town up close with swings, water tower, a grassy park . . .

HEY! Is this supposed to be Kentwood, Louisiana?

Deep Meaning: This is definitely Brit's ode to "uninterrupted love" (something she says she doesn't have much time for these days). She dreams of her BF snuggling her — but then ends up alone on a swing. Britney says, "It talks about your first love and, you know, every girl can relate to that."

Fashion Statements: Hats — brown or furry; a lovely lace-up top; and denim.

Hairy Stuff: Brit's got an up-do . . . d'oh!

Dance Track: Not much here — this is Brit as actor — she's showing more of her sentimental moves. Awwww . . . it's gonna make you cry!

Love Line: Being wrapped and snuggled in a blanket like the guy in that video.

What You Didn't Know: This is one of Britney's favorite tunes on her album — one of the first songs she did when she was signed by Jive.

What Else You Didn't Know: This was the first video Madonna "supposedly" ever saw Britney perform in! When Madonna was appearing on MTV's *TRL* countdown, she watched Britney singing her "broken heart" out! Madonna's reaction? She said, "Well, now I know what this is all about." Do you think they'll ever do a duet?

Vid-stumpers! What flowers are on the "Welcome" billboard in town?

Sunflowers!

Rate It! Any number from 1 to 10:
___Cool Factor
___ Brit's a BABE!
___ Hotties Here!
___ Love the Song
___Turn Off da Tube!

Oops! . . . I Did It Again

Setting: Britney struts around in a "heavenly" red vinyl catsuit! She's inside Universal Studios in Hollywood, California. Director Nigel Dick turned an ordinary soundstage into a space-age set where Earth meets Mars.
Deep Meaning: Britney wants to RULE the galaxy. (But you know she already does!)
Fashion Statement: Astronauts and fire-eaters
Hairy Stuff: Check out Britney's out-of-this-world hair extensions!
Dance Track: Blast off! Britney's dancing *everywhere* in this one. She shakes her stuff on the floor

and in the air! The interplanetary pop queen was filmed doing trapeze flips against a "green screen." In post-production, an editor put a computerized Mars background in where the "green" was. Now Britney's doing super-fast flips in *midair*!

Love Line: Britney says it took major "acting" to play the part of a not-so-innocent, super-flirty Mars queen in *Oops!* . . . because in real life she's a romantic who gets "really, really shy" when she meets guys.

What You Didn't Know: You read it on page 39 about how a camera konked Britney on the head during the *Oops!* shoot . . . but what you may not have heard was that Britney needed *four* stitches when treated by paramedics since she was bleeding and had a mild concussion. Ouch!

You Won't Believe This: After being treated for her injury, Britney bounced right back to the set to finish the filming later that same day. Britney's mother wanted her to relax, but hardworking Britney wanted to keep on singing and dancing.

Vid-stumpers! At the end of the video, the astronaut hands Britney a special gift. Britney says, "I thought the old lady dropped it in the ocean at the end?" What movie is she "secretly" referring to?

Titanic. The "special gift" is supposed to be the necklace Rose drops into the sea at the end of that flick.

Rate It! Any number from 1 to 10:
___Cool Factor
___ Brit's a BABE!
___ Hotties Here!
___ Love the Song
___Turn Off da Tube!

Don't miss her home videos! *Number One Time Out With Britney Spears* collects Britney's first three music videos and day-in-the-life footage. After going multiplatinum, it hit number two on *Billboard*'s video chart. It would *definitely* make a good gift for a new fan . . . but does it have enough stuff to keep die-hard fans fascinated? *Number Two* features similar interviews and exclusive chat with the teen queen *plus* full-length videos of *From the Bottom of My Broken Heart* and *Born to Make You Happy*. This video has more to offer Brit's BIGGEST fans, since the *Born to Make You Happy* video was originally released in Europe only. Can you say . . . collectible?

CHAPTER 11

And the Winner Is . . .

"At awards shows I'm usually nervous because of the celebrities in the audience. It's a little bit more intimidating."

(*Nickelodeon* magazine)

After the touring . . . after all the "stuff" . . . Britney's got her eyes on the prize!

Her album's sweet love songs and funky, up-tempo dance numbers made everyone sit up and notice. In 1999, . . . *Baby One More Time* couldn't stop winning awards and setting records. According to *Forbes* magazine, Britney's earnings totaled more than fifteen million dollars in 1999. This eighteen-year-old pop princess means business when it comes to winning music praise.

Of course, she still says she's awestruck by the Hollywood folks who hand out the awards. . . .

Welcome to the Award Zone

American Music Awards
Winner: Favorite New Artist (Pop Rock); Nominated for: Favorite Female Artist

Blockbuster 2000 Awards
Nominated for: Favorite Female New Artist, Favorite CD

Canada's Much-Music Video Awards
Winner: People's Choice Category for International Artist

1999 Eurochart Hot 100 Singles for the Year
Winner: ". . . Baby One More Time" (Jive) stayed steady at number three

Germany's Comet Awards
Winner: Best International Newcomer

Germany's Echo Awards:
Nominated for: Best New Artist

The Grammy Awards
Nominated for: Best New Artist, Best Female Pop Vocal Performance

MTV 1999 Video Awards
Nominated for: Best Pop Video, Best Female Video, Best Choreography in a Video

MTV Europe Music Awards
Winner: Best Female Artist, Best Pop Artist, Breakthrough Artist, and Best Song ". . . Baby One More Time."

Nickelodeon's 13th Annual Kids' Choice Awards
Winner: Favorite female singer

***Smash Hits* Magazine (UK)**
Winner of five reader awards: Best Female Solo Star, Best Dancer, Best Dressed, Best Haircut, and . . . get this . . . Best Fancied Female! ("Fancied," of course, meaning she's adorable and people like her lots!)

Young Star Awards
Winner: Best Young Recording Artist

Britney Spears: Record-Breaker!

As of spring 2000 . . .

- The album . . . *Baby One More Time* was certified twelve times platinum — and climbing!
- The album . . . *Baby One More Time* had eighteen million copies sold worldwide
- The album . . . *Baby One More Time* continues to be the best-selling record by a teen ever

In the history books . . .

- The album . . . *Baby One More Time* is the first album to stay at number one for six weeks since the soundtrack from *Titanic* held the crown for sixteen weeks in the first half of 1998.
- Britney Spears is the youngest female in *Billboard* magazine history to simultaneously debut a number-one single and a number-one album.

- Britney Spears is the first new act since Kris Kross in 1992 to score simultaneous number-one spots with a first album and single.
- Britney Spears is the first artist to ever jump into the number-one spot on the Hot 100 and *Billboard* 200 at the same time.
- Britney is the all-time record winner for winning the most MTV Europe awards ever. She beat out Madonna, Lauryn Hill, the Backstreet Boys, Ricky Martin, TLC, and Jennifer Lopez in different categories — wooooow!

What's in a Name . . .

- Britney Spears is the first name with the most downloads on AOL Keyword — and the fifth most popular search term on the entire net!

CHAPTER 12
Fashion Plate

"People come to my house and they're like 'Lord!'
'Cause when I'm at home the last thing I want to do
is put a lick of makeup on. I'm totally a bum."
(*Teen People*)

Some people say she's the real down-to-earth deal, while other people can't get past her tube tops and tight tees. One thing is for sure: Britney Spears has a style that's all her own — and she's not changing for anyone. With . . . *Baby One More Time* she made a new kind of schoolgirl look . . . with *Oops! . . . I Did It Again,* she's trying something different altogether . . . and who knows what's next!

Named one of *People* magazine's Fifty Most Beautiful People of 1999, this teen sensation is proud of her body — and proud of her values. Forget the waif look here! Strong, healthy, and beautiful is in with Britney. She has a healthy routine to match her healthy attitude about her body — and she's stickin' with it.

Her pre-concert workout consists of one hundred crunches and twenty-five sit-ups — every time she gets ready to go onstage. Upper body and abs are her main targets. She told *In Style* magazine: "I don't like to work out because my legs get bulky. Dancing makes me leaner." Of course, dancing almost every night would keep anyone in shape. She doesn't need to work out beyond that. She admits the thing she needs that she can't get is . . . sleep! "With all this traveling I don't have time to exercise, and when I'm not doing anything, I'm sleeping," she told MTV.

I Haven't Got a Thing To Wear!

How does she look soooooo good?

Britney has a stylist to help her decide what to wear to major events like the American Music Awards or the Grammy Awards. For example, at the 1999 Grammy's she wore a gorgeous white dress with matching fur wrap and looked elegant! She actually got kudos for her fine look, too, from fashion magazines all over. Wouldn't it be great to have your own personal stylist?

"We took her from the mall and put her on the runway," Brit's too-cool video fashion director, Hayley Hill, said. "We raised her fashion consciousness a notch!"

What else does Britney believe as far as fashion goes?

- Hair extensions come in handy when she's going for a more sophisticated look. She also uses them to get more body into her fine hair. Britney also likes to try new 'dos whenever she gets the chance. She experimented with crimped hair at the American Music Awards and she wears trendy "on top of her head" ponytails in her videos.
- She has a small cross decorated with rhinestones that she wears everywhere.
- She collects diamond jewelry — and that's why fans can see two little diamond studs in her ears. Classic style!
- Britney buys into anything that mixes girly and feminine with strong colors and textures. Check out her new look for the 2000 *Oops!* tour — wow!
- She's a sneaker addict. Britney admits to owning Skechers in all different col-

ors and styles. (She claims to have more than thirty pairs!)

- Britney can't leave home without her dark eyeliner, seashell-colored peach matte lipstick, and shimmering powders.

Fashion Ch-ch-changes

Britney's come a long way from the days of the *MMC* and she's still figuring it all out. One thing she knows for certain: She needs to keep changing her look until she gets it juuuuust right! Brit's evolving, growing, and changing just like her fans.

Getting great clothes for the videos ends up being excellent for Britney, since she gets to keep all the clothes she wears onscreen. Just don't expect to see Brit prancing around in the . . . *Baby One More Time* school girl outfit. She's leaving those leggings . . . and those feathery pink hair elastics — on the set. She also has a traveling wardrobe for her shows on the road. Would you believe that Britney changes clothes at least six times during every single concert? She keeps extra sets of the same clothes she needs for back-to-back shows.

The *In Style* magazine editor says about Britney: "With her dancer's body and muscular physique, Britney likes things to hug her figure. She gravitates towards the street-inspired styles of Tommy Hilfiger, A/X, and Abercrombie & Fitch when she's hanging out and Calvin Klein and Donna Karan for dressier times."

Fashion Advice from Brit's Closet

1. Skirts that hit below the knee don't flatter Britney best. But she likes miniskirts. Try different lengths to see what works best on you!
2. Forget about navel showoffs! Gradually, everyone is getting "over the whole belly thing," Britney admits. Still, you can still catch a glimpse of her abs in those videos . . . plus tight tees still jampack her closet and suitcases when she travels. Show off your tummy (only if you feel comfortable).
3. Keep accessories simple. Britney's diamond earrings are the just-right, simple fashion statement. Rhinestones will give you that certain sparkle . . .
4. Clothes aren't the whole thing! Be proud of your body — and who you are. Britney believes

that keeping your head held high is half the fashion statement. Stand tall.

5. Who cares what you're wearing when you look like you've been up all night? Get your beauty sleep. Right now Brit's back on the road — and she's often not snoozin' as much as she'd like. Whenever she can catch forty winks she does. She says it makes all the difference to the way she looks — and feels.

Final Fashion Thought

Although fans can spot Britney sporting the coolest clothes, there is a giant part of the pop queen who doesn't care a stitch about what she wears! "I don't care what people say about my hair or my looks, but when they start in on my performance, that's when it hurts."

Translation: Britney likes to get decked out in wild clothes for performing . . . but all she really cares about is that she does a great job singing, dancing, and making her fans happy!

CHAPTER 13

Boy-oh-Boy

"I want a guy I can be totally honest with and make me laugh. Most important, he's gotta be secure with himself because I'm on the road a lot and around other guys and the last thing I want to have to worry about is a jealous, insecure guy."

(*Jump* magazine)

If you listen to Britney's first album, you know what she's thinking about . . . three of the songs have the word "heart" in the title! She's usually got love on the brain — but traveling and performing doesn't leave her much time to actually date. "When I'm on tour, I wake up early and travel nonstop. There's just no time for anything!"

When asked if she used to go out more while she lived back home, Britney quickly says, "Nooooo! Not at all! I never dated." But then she admits she did have a first love back in Louisiana named Reg. She saw him for almost two years, but they've been split up for a while now. Her concert and promotion schedule made it too hard for her to keep up the relationship. It was just too tough to only talk on the phone. Plus, she confided in one interview, "Right now I want to go on a lot of dates, without anything serious."

Hmmmmmm . . . what's the real deal with Britney and boys? Would she like to hook up with someone in show business? "I think it would help a lot. Of course, if I met somebody at McDonald's and I fell in love with him, I'd have to go with my heart. But it would help being in the same industry, because you know what that person is going through, scheduling-wise. Somebody else might not realize I'm really busy all day long."

According to the media, fans would swear Britney is dating all the 'N Sync boys behind each other's backs. Britney says those kind of tabloid tales leave her in tears — and when she's really not dating, she wishes people would just believe her. Still, there are plenty of creative ideas about who Britney might be seeing now . . . or in the future.

Britney's Rate-a-Date

'N Sync's J.C. (Joshua) Chasez?

He's twenty-three — a little older than Brit's typical date. But J.C. has some thoughts on the teen queen: "Guys are into her because she's cute and girls like her because she's not trying too hard." Do they have anything in common? They both chew their nails. Eeeeuw — not too romantic.

'N Sync's Justin Timberlake?

Britney + Justin is the rumor that won't quit. Any number of sources claim to have seen Brit and Justin in a clinging clutch backstage, at parties, and other hot spots. But the answer from both camps was always a loud: NOTHING GOING ON HERE. Brit said in *USA Today*, "People are always gonna say stuff so they can make some money. He's a real cutie patootie, but we're just friends."

But a big revelation came in May, when Brit told *Rolling Stone*, "I wouldn't say we're boyfriend and girlfriend. We hook up every once in a while, and we'll talk . . . We just hang out." But do they ever smooch? "Sometimes," Britney answered. Then she screams, "Oh my God! I'm blushing."

As for Justin, he admits that "Britney's a good friend. I've known her since I was twelve . . . I choose to hang with people who are down-to-earth and very humble and she's definitely one of them." He's not confirming — or denying, it would seem.

LFO's Rich Cronin?

Maybe something got heated up in their spring 2000 tour . . . but it's not likely. He's dated Jennifer Love Hewitt. He's commented in the past that he "likes" Brit, but that could mean anything. Do they have anything in common? They both have lived in Orlando. Yawn.

Boyz and Girlz United's Robbie Carrico?

They're friends. End of story. They worked together on the road and got to be pals. He escorted her to premiere of pal Melissa Joan Hart's *Drive Me Crazy*. Do they have anything in common? He has a Yorkshire terrier, just like Brit. His pup's name is Mickey, and she was on the *New Mickey Mouse Club*. That's cute!

Actor Ben Affleck?

Britney is crushing. In a major way. Quotes from her (on the record): "My dream is to make a movie and have a love scene with Ben Affleck." "He doesn't have my number, but I have his . . . totally!" "We're not dating even though I wish!" They did have a luncheon together once with some friends — at Planet Hollywood. Brit used it as an opportunity to gush some more. "I told him I wanted him to direct one of my videos, as long as he was my love interest!" Do they have anything in common? No.

Actor Brad Pitt?
Brit's you-drive-me-crazy crush number two. "There's only one guy for me and that's Brad Pitt. I just have to get rid of Jennifer Aniston." She's kidding, of course. Do Brit and Pitt *really* have anything in common? Both were born Sagittarius.

England's Prince William?
Was there an e-mail relationship or wasn't there? Apparently, she sent him a CD with a note and some other stuff, but according to *People* magazine, they haven't actually met yet (as of early 2000). Britney doesn't know why these rumors get started. "He's very cute and sweet, but people blow things out of proportion." Do they have anything in common? They've both met Scary Spice.

CHAPTER 14
Girl Talk

"My audience looks at me like a girlfriend. That's how I was trying to portray it on stage — like, 'All of us girls out there!' Instead of being like, I don't know, 'I've got a man and duh-duh-duh.' I didn't want the jealousy thing."

(Entertainment Weekly)

Britney's friends arc very important to her. She looks for "honesty and, of course, sweetness" in her closest gal pals. Most important, she also tries to never let life on thc road interfere with her friendships back home. That can be difficult, especially when she's headed out on a new "world" tour. She told *Girl's Life* magazine, "We keep in touch, call each other, and keep up with the gossip." Can you imagine her long distance phone bill?

Her pals love to trade "Best of Brit" stories . . . which usually means they're poking fun at their favorite buddy. (With kindness in their hearts, of course!) Friend Tara laughs when she tells a story of how Britney blew it once at a school track meet. "It was her first year running track and she was at her first track meet, and everybody got on the line, the starting blocks, and they shot the gun and she just stood there! She didn't know what the gunshot meant!" In an MTV interview, Britney admitted that the story was true, as embarrassing as it was.

Some of Britney's best memories of her friends revolve around her earliest driving experiences — although they didn't involve shopping. "It would rain and we would go outside and we'd all get our go-carts and we'd put on the trashiest clothes in the world and go mud riding! We'd be drenched in mud but it was so much fun!"

Now Britney hops in her new car and takes off. In 2000, she traded in a Mercedes SL500 convertible she bought after the first leg of her tour for a hot-looking Jaguar. Where does she go? Where does any regular teenager go? Britney told *Jump* magazine, "Let's just say I know my way around a mall."

That's right, the number-one thing on the list of friend activities for Britney's bunch has to be . . . SHOPPING! "When I have some time I do my schoolwork but like if I am home, I just wanna be with my friends and go to the beach . . . and I love shopping." The only thing that's different about shopping with Britney is that she can afford to take her friends on shopping sprees. Ever since she got her license, whenever Britney is home, she and her friends cruise around, laugh, and shop till they drop.

The best part about Brit's hometown friends: They keep her honest — and down to earth. Her BFF Erin says, "I love her. She's like a sister, she's great and I think she'll always do real well."

Happy Eighteenth Birthday, Britney!

On December 2, 1999, Britney celebrated her eighteenth birthday in New York City with her best friends from Kentwood. The bash was held at an exclusive club called Halo. How did it feel to hit the big 1-8? Britney confessed to *USA Today*, "I still feel like a teenager in some ways, but there is somethin' about being eighteen. You feel like you're more of an adult."

She told *Nickelodeon* magazine the inside story about her birthday event. "Some of my girlfriends from back home . . . came up to New York. We got dressed together, my makeup artist did their makeup, and then we took a limousine to my party. When they started singing 'Happy Birthday' I just lost it. All of those memories of the whole year came back to me and I started crying. I was such a goob!"

There were stars at the b-day bash, too, like her escort, pal Robbie Carrico (from Boyz and Girlz United), the guys from 'N Sync, Ja Rule, actress Tara Reid, and Pras. But it was Britney's hometown buds who got most of her undivided attention. Together they ate a scrumptious chocolate birthday cake with raspberry filling. It even had a buttercream frosting picture of Britney on top.

The best gift of the night? Her record label, Jive, gave her a millennium diamond necklace in a Tiffany setting. She wears it now wherever she goes.

Britney Spears versus Christina Aguilera

You can't talk "girl talk" without getting into the whole Britney versus Christina rivalry. In early 2000 *USA Today* featured a comparison chart showing the two stars. Each pop princess has a group of fans that fiercely defends their singer. Fans say that Britney is "the next Madonna," while Christina is "the next Mariah Carey."

How did all this competition begin?

Christina has been traveling and performing all

over the world since she was very small. Her dad is in the military, so the family moved around a lot. Mom is a violinist and pianist who toured Europe when the kids were younger. Believe it or not, Christina has lived in Japan, Florida, Texas, and other places.

Christina didn't grow up in a small town, but other than that . . . she and Britney have shared very similar performing experiences.

- Both stars "wanted to perform as long as they could remember."
- Both competed in talent shows and pageants as young girls.
- Both appeared on *Star Search*: Christina at age eight; Britney at age eleven. (Christina lost; Britney won one episode).
- Both have sung the national anthem at a sporting event.
- Both landed a spot on *The New Mickey Mouse Club* at the same time — same cast.
- Both recorded a "demo tape" singing at least one Whitney Houston song.
- Both singers have albums that have

climbed the pop charts — as well as sin-gles that have been featured on suc-cessful movie sound tracks. Christina recorded a song for Disney's *Mulan* and *Pokemon: The First Movie* sound track; Britney was featured on the *Drive Me Crazy* as well as *Pokemon: The First Movie* sound tracks.

- Both singers have worked with song-ballad writer Diane Warren.
- Both have December birthdays. Christina is December 18; Britney is December 2.
- Both have one brother and one sister. Christina's are step-siblings.
- Both are blonds, love to shop, and like to show off their belly buttons.

The truth is that back in the days of *MMC*, Christina and Britney were actually close friends. Britney said: "Christina is a beautiful person inside. She's very honest, down-to-earth, and a good friend." Christina said that Britney could "always make me smile and feel good about myself. . . . We love to get new clothes, we both kid around a lot, love to go to the movies!"

Britney said about her "rival": "We get compared a lot because we're both the same age and our backgrounds are similar." Christina agreed that the whole thing was blown out of proportion. "It's frustrating being compared to Britney because we are two very different artists. We both dance and sing but people have not had enough time to realize that there is a huge difference between us. If she wants to go and do something . . . I think I will want to do the opposite."

What's Your PQQ (Pop Queen Quotient)?

Whether the fans like it or not, Britney will always being linked to someone — for better or for worse. If it's not rumors about Christina, it's a made-up story about Britney's newest love interest, or it's an MTV video showdown between some other stars.

Britney may be the true original, but sometimes it can be hard to tell the pop queens apart. What is your Pop Queen IQ? Are you a Pop Star Smarty or a Diva Dunce?

On the next pages are fifteen multiple choice questions about today's hottest pop princesses. Can you answer all fifteen correctly? Fans will find the answers at the back of this book.

1. She loves to give "Sweet Kisses" to Nick Lachey of 98°.
   a) Britney Spears
   b) Jessica Simpson
   c) Christina Aguilera

2. She was nicknamed "the American Anthem Girl" around Orlando, where she lives.
   a) Britney Spears
   b) Christina Aguilera
   c) Mandy Moore

3. Her dad is from Ecuador, South America, but she doesn't speak Spanish.
   a) Christina Aguilera
   b) Hoku
   c) Mandy Moore

4. These two were both rejected by *The New Mickey Mouse Club* at some point.
   a) Jessica & Christina
   b) Christina & Britney
   c) Jessica & Britney

5. This name means "star" in Hawaiian.
   a) Hoku
   b) Aguilera
   c) Britney

6. She is in negotiations to have her own TV show on the WB.
   a) Britney Spears
   b) Jessica Simpson
   c) Mandy Moore

7. She likes to shop.
   a) Christina & Mandy
   b) Jessica & Britney
   c) both a & b

8. She ripped her pants onstage at a Madison Square Garden, New York concert.
   a) Jessica Simpson
   b) Britney Spears
   c) Christina Aguilera

9. She's appeared at the White House and at Opryland.
   a) Hoku
   b) Jessica Simpson
   c) Mandy Moore

10. She helps sponsor an orphanage in Mexico each summer.
    a) Christina Aguilera
    b) Hoku
    c) Jessica Simpson

11. Her dad was a famous ukelele player.
    a) Britney Spears
    b) Hoku
    c) Jessica Simpson

12. She auditioned for her record label singing a Whitney Houston song.
    a) Christina Aguilera
    b) Britney Spears
    c) both a & b

13. She's appeared onstage in a musical or play.
    a) Mandy & Christina
    b) Christina & Britney
    c) Mandy & Britney

14. Her dad is a preacher.
    a) Mandy Moore
    b) Britney Spears
    c) Jessica Simpson

15. They're all blond, but only this girl sings a song about it.
    a) Christina Aguilera
    b) Hoku
    c) Jessica Simpson

CHAPTER 15

Shhh! Spears Secrets & Embarrassing Stuff

How Embarrassing!

Like all fans, Britney has been mortified more than once. Unfortunately, for her, embarrassments tend to happen in front of millions of people. Gotta hate that! Here are some of the worst of those moments — in Britney's own words . . .

The Mole Truth

"I had the worst embarrassing makeup moment in front of a whole stadium. I was all set to walk on-stage to open for 'N Sync in Dallas, when I noticed a large spot on my cheek. It was a pimple. I covered it with eyeliner and made a mole, but then midway through the show, that smeared because I had been sweating!"

The Headset

"My worst moment happened . . . in Fort Wayne, Indiana. I was singing and my headset and mic were connected to this (receiver) that was taped on my body and it all just fell off. I put it back on really quickly but it was so embarrassing. Thank goodness it was during my last song. If it had been at the beginning, I would have died."

The Cupcake

"One time I came on after the group B*witched . . . and when I got onstage there was a cupcake on the stage and of course, I fell. I had these major platform shoes and all of a sudden I slipped and down I went. I was so embarrassed! There was an arena of people there looking at me, flat on my butt."

Would You Believe . . .

Britney Is Ultra-Sensitive

"People tend to think someone in the public eye is not normal and say some things that hurt my feelings. I wish they would stop." (*NY Daily News*)

Britney Worries Like Crazy

"I worry a lot. Like I'll be in bed at night and I'll just think of the stupidest things, I'm so paranoid. I want to quit biting my nails too, it's a bad habit."

Britney Gets Overwhelmed — Wouldn't You?

On the fans: "They're just, like, crazy. It's flattering to a certain extent but sometimes they get a little overbearing and you're like "Stay back!" (*Entertainment Weekly*)

Other Britney Spears Secrets

- Britney has two impossible wishes: "I wish I were taller and I wish my hair was thicker."
- Britney had her navel pierced in early 2000 with a silver-and-turquoise ring — over her mom's objections.
- She also has a tattoo of a small black-winged fairy down by the base of her spine — also over her mom's objections. Britney got the tattoo in New York after returning from a Christmas 1999 trip to Hawaii with friends.

- Britney says that if she could change one body part it would be her toes. She says they are so UGLY!
- She bites her nails . . . bad!
- She's super-cranky when she doesn't get enough sleep!
- She has a HUGE pet peeve: Fake people who try to take advantage of others.
- Britney failed her driver's test the first time around (because she admitted she did not study!).
- When Britney called MTV's *TRL* to announce her spring 2000 tour, she informed viewers that she just had her wisdom teeth removed!
- Britney had a crummy first kiss: "It was okay during it, but the next day the boy ignored me. And I liked him soooo much."
- Britney's new teacup terrier needs some serious "on the road" potty training. Mom admits the puppy was having a few accidents . . . every day. (But Brit still loves curling up and sleeping with her!)

- Lynne says that Britney is constantly changing the CD and tape player in the car when she drives. Sound familiar?
- She wore clear braces — and a clunky, gross retainer before that! Ugh!
- Britney admits that when she was laid up with her knee injury in 1999, she went into Cartier (an expensive jeweler in New York) and tried on an $80,000 ring! What was so bad was the fact that she was wearing bedroom slippers and in a wheelchair at the time — and hadn't taken a bath in two days!
- Britney admits that no matter how famous she gets, she is still TOTALLY starstruck herself. She remembers one time: "I was in New York with my friend Felicia and I was like, 'Oh, my God that's Tori Spelling!' She was walking down the street with a guy she's dating on the show. I was totally freaked out. I also saw Prince and Scary Spice. I am totally starstruck."

CHAPTER 16

Random Facts from the Encyclopedia "Brit"annica!

FULL NAME: Britney Jean Spears

BORN: December 2, 1981 on the border of Kentwood, Louisiana and McComb, Misssissippi

RIGHTIE OR LEFTIE: She's officially right-handed but she favors her left side for dance and sports.

INNIE OR OUTIE: Innie! C'mon — you only see it in every photo!

NICKNAME: Brit-Brit, Boo Boo

HER FAMILY: Mom Lynne, Dad Jamie, Little Sister Jamie-Lynn, and Older Brother Brian

HER BODYGUARD: Rob

HER DANCERS: TJ, Andre, Charissa, and Tania — go everywhere with Brit. "They are my best friends in the world!"

BIGGEST FEAR: Flying. "When I went to Sweden

and to Singapore, it was my first time out of the country and I was scared to death to fly on that plane."

COLLECTS: Fairies (like her tattoo), diamond jewelry

DRINK: Ice cream mixed with cappuccino

CEREAL: Cap'n Crunch and Cocoa Puffs (a toss up)

ICE CREAM: Ben & Jerry's Cookie Dough with Pralines & Cream as second favorite.

EATING AT HOME: Pasta, mom's homemade baked chicken, and hot dogs

EATING ON THE ROAD: "I love airplane food. Most people hate it, but I love those little turkey sandwiches and the little bags of chips."

FAST FOOD: Taco Bell, Carl's Jr., Dunkin Donuts, Waffle House, White Castle, Starbucks (she loves junk food!). "Every once in a while, like after a late drive, me and my dancers beg JT our driver to take us to a twenty-four-hour White Castle or Waffle House or something like that."

HIGH SCHOOL: First, Parklane Academy. Now, correspondence courses at the University of Nebraska.

SCHOOL SUBJECT: English and history (she also speaks a little Spanish)

WORST SUBJECT: Geometry/math/trigonometry

BEST TEACHER: Mrs. Hughes, in third grade

COLLEGE MAJOR: Someday! Business or communications

MOVIE GROWIN' UP: *The Wizard of Oz* ("I have Dorothy stuff all over my room!")

TEEN MOVIE: *Titanic*, *Steel Magnolias*

BEST DISNEY CHARACTER: Goofy or Daisy

BEST RIDES AT DISNEY WORLD: Rockin' Rollercoaster and Space Mountain

AUTHOR: Danielle Steele

BOOK: *The Horse Whisperer* and any romance novels!!!

MAGAZINE: *Cosmopolitan*

HOBBY: Reading trashy novels and going shopping

SPORTS TEAMS: Chicago Bulls, New York Yankees

HER DREAM DATE: "A guy taking me to a really romantic, candlelight dinner and then he'd take me somewhere with a pretty view."

MOVIE STAR GUY: Ben Affleck, Brad Pitt, and Tom Cruise

MOVIE STAR GAL: Meg Ryan, Sandra Bullock

TV SHOW: *Friends* or *Felicity* (and yes, she even is a fan of WWF!)

SONG: "Purple Rain" by Prince (a/k/a the Artist)

SINGERS: Mariah Carey, Aerosmith, Prince, the Backstreet Boys, Third Eye Blind (she likes the Top 40, just like her fans)

IN HER CD PLAYER: TLC, Lauryn Hill, Madonna's *Immaculate Collection*

INSTRUMENT SHE WISHES SHE COULD PLAY: Guitar

SONG SHE'D SING FIRST AT KARAOKE: Anything from *Grease*

IF SHE WERE A SPICE GIRL, SHE'D BE . . . Baby Spice! (or should that be ". . . Baby One More Time" Spice?)

IF SHE WERE A SUPERHERO, SHE'D BE . . . the Pink Power Ranger!

IF SHE WERE AN ANIMAL, SHE'D BE . . . A bird so she could fly, or a puppy dog!

BEST PLACE TO TRAVEL: England, Bahamas, Hawaii

DREAM TOUR: Headlining with Michael Jackson

BEST FAMOUS FRIEND: Edwin McCain (hit singer of "I'll Be")

WEIRDEST FAN REQUEST: "Please sign my . . . ?" Someone wanted her to sign his body!

ON HER VOICE: "Before a show, I love to drink hot water with lemon and honey. I go into a quiet room and scream until my voice opens up."

ON WASTING TIME: On tour bus she plays games called Questions — "everybody writes down a question on a piece of paper you go around in a circle and have to pick one."

TOP THREE THINGS THAT ARE IMPORTANT: God, my family, and happiness

WHERE SHE'LL BE IN TWENTY YEARS: She told fans on an MSN chat, "I'd like to have a big house and three kids and just be a mom. Of course, I'll let my kids go into show business if they want to."

Making a Mooooove into Milk Ads!

Brit sported sportswear for Tommy Hilfiger ads and showed up talkin' on the phone in a groovy got milk? ad when her first album came out. The first Britney Spears got milk? ad read: "Baby, one more time isn't enough. Nine out of ten girls don't get enough calcium. It takes about four glasses of milk every day. So when I finish this glass, fill it up, baby. Three more times."

Cool fact: She's a rare singing star because she has a second milk ad — which ran summer 2000 to tie into her second whirlwind North American tour sponsored by . . . who else? Got milk! The second ad shows a li'l girl in a totally cute tutu. She's standing alongside Brit as a grown woman — in a stylin' black-and-pink outfit with leather pants. The caption read, "Grow up." Britney sure has!

CHAPTER 17
FAN-tastic

No matter how many hours Britney is out on the road touring, she always comes back to the most important thing of all: the fans. She knows the fans are what makes everything possible.

In July 1999, she and her mom went to the Hammond Square Mall in Louisiana where she judged a Britney Spears contest. All the girls there — hundreds of contestants — showed up in Britney-esque schoolgirl uniforms to sing ". . . Baby One More Time" karaoke style. No matter how many times she sees fans acting this way, she says she will never get used to it.

But today, almost two years after hitting the *Billboard* magazine number-one spots, she takes it all in stride. She admits that she's a starstruck fan herself. "I'd be just like those fans if I met a singer or performer I liked, I'd scream and be speechless."

That's the best thing about Britney. In her heart, she's a fan too . . . of you.

ONE FINE FAN: Sheena Ruiz who got to be on MTV's FAN-atic! — chosen from almost one thousand videotaped pleas. Brit loved hanging out with her — like a girlfriend. "By the end of the visit, I felt so close to her!"

ONE UN-FINE FAN: A toss up between the guy who came knocking on the family's front door — and a family who caught mom Lynne off guard one day just poppin' in the driveway to "say hi!"

WOULD SHE DATE A FAN? She told an AOL chat room, "I don't know. Maybe if I met the person. Sure. All that matters would be if I dig the person and I loved the person, you know, I would. But it's so hard to meet anyone when I am so busy!"

GREATEST ADVICE TO HER FANS: "If (you) have a major love for music or singing or dancing or whatever it is, (you) should definitely go for it, cause God's given (you) the talent and (you) should use it and express it. But there is a lot of hard work involved, so just be prepared for that. I think God has plans for everyone and I'm just thankful this is his plan for me."

MORE FAN-TASTIC ADVICE: "Life is short. Don't waste it." Britney knows what she wants, and she goes for it . . . and thinks everyone else should, too!

Wanna Know What's New?

When you need to know what is going on with Britney as it happens, the best place to check is the web.

HER OFFICIAL SITE: http://www.britney.com

THE MUSIC AND VIDEO SCOOP: MTV devotes web gallery pages to what is new and happening with Britney. Check it out! http://www.mtv.com

How You Can Get in Touch:
    Britney Beat
    Dept. Fan Mail
    P.O. Box 192730
    San Francisco, CA 94119-2730

Britney Spears
c/o Jive Records
137–139 West 25th Street
New York, NY 10001

Answers to What's Your PQQ (Pop Queen Quotient)?

1. She loves to give "Sweet Kisses" to Nick Lachey of 98°.
b) Jessica Simpson — she sang a romantic duet with him, "Where You Are."
2. She was nicknamed "the American Anthem Girl" around Orlando, where she lives.
c) Mandy Moore — she's sung at major sports events, including tennis tournaments!
3. Her dad is from Ecuador, South America, but she doesn't speak Spanish.
a) Christina Aguilera — she wants to learn the language though!
4. These two were both rejected by *The New Mickey Mouse Club* at some point.
c) Jessica & Britney — Jessica at age twelve (at her first and only audition); Britney at age eight (but as

fans know, she came back and did get on the show at age eleven).

5. This name means "star" in Hawaiian.

a) Hoku — she lives there — and was discovered by a songwriter touring Maui!

6. She is in negotiations to have her own TV show on the WB.

b) Jessica Simpson — it's a drama series.

7. She likes to shop.

c) both a & b — everyone likes to shop!

8. She ripped her pants onstage at a Madison Square Garden, New York concert.

a) Jessica Simpson — it happened when she was opening for Ricky Martin.

9. She's appeared at the White House and at Opryland.

c) Mandy Moore — she may be one of the youngest teen sensations (age sixteen), but she's done a lot in her short career.

10. She helps sponsor an orphanage in Mexico each summer.

c) Jessica Simpson — she goes there and works each summer, too.

11. Her dad was a famous ukelele player.

b) Hoku — Don Ho is her dad, and he sang a hit

song called "Tiny Bubbles." Maybe your parents or grandparents remember it? Ask 'em!

12. She auditioned for her record label singing a Whitney Houston song.

c) both a & b — Christina and Britney think Whitney Houston is the most divine diva. Christina sang "I Wanna Run to You" at her audition; and Britney sang "I Have Nothing" at hers.

13. She's appeared onstage in a musical or play.

c) Mandy & Britney — Britney was in the off-Broadway show *Ruthless,* but Mandy's the real stage veteran. She's had roles in regional theater productions like *Bye, Bye Birdie* and *Guys and Dolls.*

14. Her dad is a preacher.

c) Jessica Simpson — she takes her faith seriously, too.

15. They're all blond, but only this girl sings a song about it.

b) Hoku — her hit, "Another Dumb Blonde," from the soundtrack of the movie *Snow Day* put her on the map . . . but she's no dummy!